AN EXALTATION OF
ROMANCE
& REVELRY

To: _____

From: _____

D0108534

ALSO BY JAMES LIPTON

An Exaltation of Larks
Mirrors
An Exaltation of Larks, the Ultimate Edition
An Exaltation of Business and Finance
An Exaltation of Home and Family

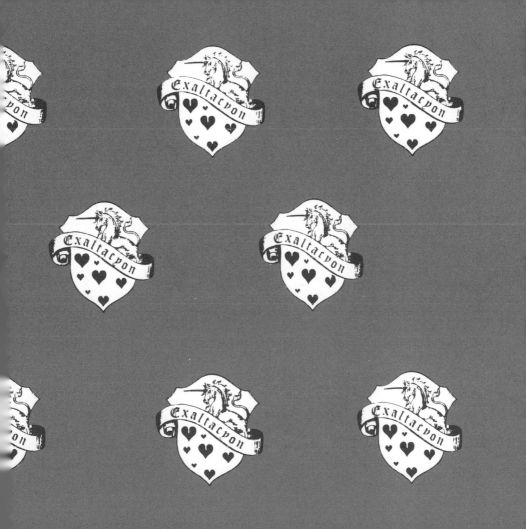

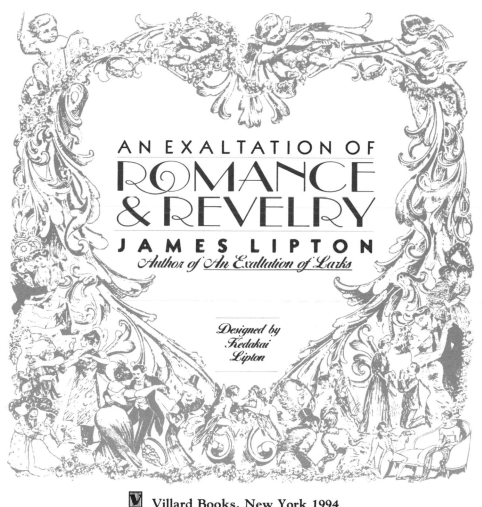

AN EXALTATION OF
ROMANCE & REVELRY

JAMES LIPTON
Author of *An Exaltation of Larks*

Designed by
Redakai
Lipton

Villard Books, New York 1994

VILLARD BOOKS is a registered trademark of Random House, Inc.

Grateful acknowledgment is made to Penguin Books USA Inc. for permission to reprint 49 terms from *An Exaltation of Larks* by James Lipton. Copyright © 1968, 1977, 1991 by James Lipton. Reprinted by permission of Viking Penguin, a division of Penguin Books USA Inc.

We wish to extend thanks to the Archives of the *New York Herald*, Paris edition, and the *International Herald Tribune*, Paris (page 10); the Library of Congress; the Bettmann Archive (page 33); the Smithsonian Institute H. T. Peters America On Stone Lithograph Collection (page 51); the Collection of the New York Historical Society (page 41); and the New York Public Library Picture Collection.

Library of Congress Cataloging-in-Publication information is available.
ISBN: 0-679-41872-5

Book and Illustration Design by Kedakai Lipton
Manufactured in the United States of America on 100% acid-free paper.
2 4 6 8 9 7 5 3
First Edition

Prelude

The English language's unique habit of assigning to groups of animals an imaginative, often witty, sometimes poetic or sardonic, but always surprising and illuminating term began in 1323 when King Edward II's huntsman, Master William Twici, undertook to codify the language of a gentleman's only peacetime occupation: hunting. Master Twici's book, written in Norman French, was called *Le Art de Venerie*, the word *venery* deriving from the same Latin sources as Venus, and referring in this case to the hunter's passionate pursuit of his quarry. Six hundred forty-five years later, there was, oddly, still no proper collective for these fascinating collectives, so, inspired by Master Twici, I selected *terms of venery* to describe the subject of my book *An Exaltation of Larks*.

An exaltation of larks is, of course, a term of venery, which is to say it is, in my opinion, the proper term for a group of larks—as opposed, say, to a *school* or *pride* of larks. If *school* and *pride* of larks sound peculiar, it's because, since the fourteenth century, the English language has retained its curious venereal habit, and most of us say a *school of fish* or *pride of lions* (or *host of angels*) without realizing we are using terms of venery invented and codified more than six hundred years ago.

Today we'd provoke snickers if we said *a herd of fish* or *a school of elephants*, but in the fifteenth century such a gaffe would have been shocking, as would have anything but *a sloth of bears, a leap of leopards, a murder of crows,* or *an exaltation of larks*—or, more precisely, *an exaltacyon of larkys*, as the Egerton Manuscript put it in 1452 (which explains the coat of arms on this and all the books in the *Exaltation* series). A young gentleman of that period had to learn by rote *all* the terms of venery, and to assist him, numerous manuscripts and books were written on the subject, each one including what the scribe or author considered to be a definitive list.

1486 was a venereal watershed, for in that year, only a decade after William Caxton introduced printing to England, the "schoolmaster printer" published *The Book of St. Albans* by Dame Juliana Barnes, with its historic list of 164 terms.

Five hundred years later, when I first sensed that *a pride of lions* and *a gaggle of geese* might be only the tip of a linguistic iceberg, I embarked on a journey that led me eventually to the Reading Room of the British Museum, where I held in my hands *The Book of St. Albans*, and, turning Dame Juliana's pages at last, discovered that, side-by-side with *a skulk of foxes*, *a labor of moles*, and *a shrewdness of apes*, were such antic inventions as *a bevy of ladies* (yes, Mr. Ziegfeld—in 1486), *a rascal of boys*, *a rage of maidens* and *an incredulity of cuckolds* (yes, Mr. Hefner—in 1486).

In a language-besotted country that was about to give birth to an age of literary genius the likes of which the world had never seen, and will probably never see again, Dame Juliana and her contemporaries had turned "science" into art, solemn pedantry into airy fantasy, and the English language into a playground without fences.

In short, the venereal *game* had been born — which inspired and emboldened me, as I snatched *a charm of finches* and *an unkindness of ravens* back from the void into which they had vanished, to invent terms of venery for our own time: *a slouch of models*, *a wince of dentists*, *a charge of shoppers*, *a shrivel of critics*, *a lot of realtors*, *a score of bachelors*, *a trance of lovers*, *a mass of Bostonians*, *a pocket of quarterbacks*, *a handful of gynecologists*, *an unction of undertakers* (in a larger group *an extreme unction of undertakers*) . . .

It was like eating peanuts: I couldn't stop. And neither, I'm happy to report, could the readers of *An Exaltation of Larks*. The book has remained in print from the day of its publication to the present, updated and expanded to the current 324-page *Ultimate Edition* by *a flood of venereal terms* from all over the world.

Ultimate became *penultimate* as I was urged and inspired to begin a new series of *Exaltations*, each focusing its quizzical gaze on a single subject. The series began with *An Exaltation of Business and Finance*, followed a few months later by *An Exaltation of Home and Family*. Now here is the next installment: *An Exaltation of Romance and Revelry*, the research for which was a special pleasure to the author and the book's designer.

As with every *Exaltation* book, this one is a cordial invitation to join me—and Dame Juliana Barnes—in the game of venery as it has been played by word lovers for nearly seven hundred years.

A trance of lovers

A gush of valentines   A hush of hopes   A rush of feelings

A blush of encounters   A brush of hands   A flush of cheeks

A crush of hugs   A mush of love letters   A slush of passions

A gawk of puppy loves

A fervor of first loves

A fever of infatuations

A caress of sweethearts
A dandle of darlings
A clutch of main squeezes

A peck of kisses *(pleasant)*
A gross of kisses *(unpleasant)*

A bevy of beauties

A bevy of ladies *pops up in 1486 in* The Book of St. Albans' *seminal list of venereal terms as the ninth term, between* a nye of pheasants *and* a bevy of roes. The Oxford English Dictionary *gives up on the origin of* bevy *with* "*Derivation and early history unknown,*" *but hazards the guess that it derives from the Old French* bevée *or* buvée, drink *or* drinking. *Make of that what you will.*

A charm of flirts

Charm *is another authentic fifteenth-century venereal term, appearing in* The Book of St. Albans *as* a charm of goldfinches.

A press of suitors

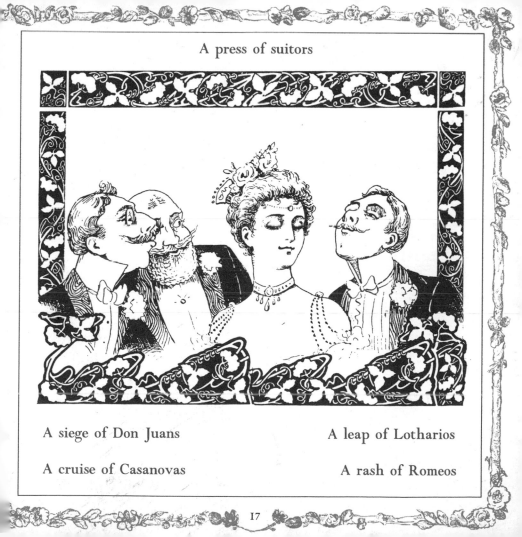

A siege of Don Juans

A cruise of Casanovas

A leap of Lotharios

A rash of Romeos

An offering of flowers
A remembrance of roses

A chest of corsages
A *beau geste* of *bijoux*

A split of Dutch treats

A skirmish of dates

A jitter of first dates

A lottery of blind dates

A company of double dates

A chill of commitments

A frostbite of cold feet

A tempest of broken promises

An avalanche of lovers' quarrels

A winter of farewells

A springtime of reconciliations

A ladder of elopements

A genuflection of proposals

A deluge of bridal showers

A debauch of bachelor parties

A glow of engagements

A gleam of engagement rings

A blizzard of invitations
A march of wedding rehearsals

REQUIREMENTS OF THE
HUSBAND

A man shall leave father and mother, and cleave to his wife. *Gen. 2. 24. Mark 10. 28.*

Let every man have his own wife. *1 Cor. 7. 2.*

Husbands shall dwell with their wives according to knowledge, giving honor unto them, as unto the weaker vessel. *1 Pet. 3. 7.*

Husbands love your wives, even as Christ loved the Church, and gave himself for it. *Eph. 5. 25.*

So ought man to love their wives as their own bodies, he that loveth his wife, loveth himself. *Eph. 5. 28. 33.*

Let the husband render unto the wife due benevolence. *1 Cor. 7. 3. See also 1 Cor. 1. 33.*

If a husband provide not for his own (wife and children,) he is worse than an infidel. *1 Tim. 5. 8.*

A man shall cheer up his wife. *Deut. 24. 5.*

Husbands love your wives, and be not bitter against them. *Col. 3. 19.*

Art thou bound to a wife, seek not to be loosed. *1 Cor. 7. 27.*

Marriage is honorable in all. *Heb. 13. 4.*

Let not the husband put away his wife. *1 Cor. 7. 11.*

Let none deal treacherously against the wife of his youth. God hateth putting away. *Mal. 2. 15. 16.*

It is a wicked act that a man should gain the heart of a woman, and then forsake his wife.

" Whom God hath joined together, let no man put asun

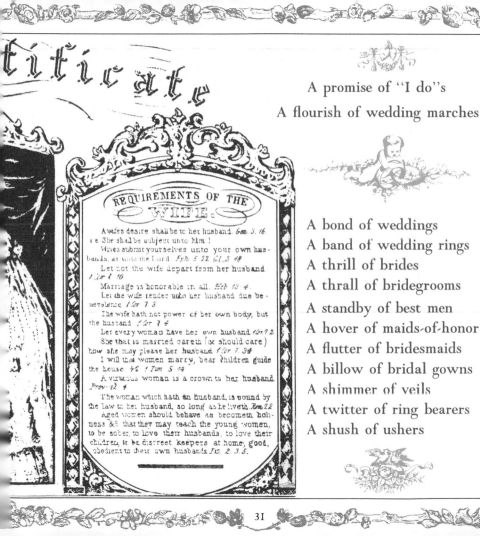

REQUIREMENTS OF THE
WIFE.

A wife's desire shall be to her husband. *Gen. 3. 16.*
i e She shall be subject unto him.!

Wives submit yourselves unto your own husbands, as unto the Lord. *Eph. 5. 22. Col. 3. 18.*

Let not the wife depart from her husband.
1 Cor. 7. 10.

Marriage is honorable in all. *Heb. 13. 4.*

Let the wife render unto her husband due benevolence *1 Cor. 7. 3.*

The wife hath not power of her own body, but
the husband *1 Cor. 7. 4.*

Let every woman have her own husband *1Cor. 7. 2.*

She that is married careth (or should care)
how she may please her husband *1 Cor. 7. 34.*

I will that women marry, bear children guide
the house *1 Tim. 5. 14.*

A virtuous woman is a crown to her husband.
Prov. 12. 4.

The woman which hath an husband, is bound by
the law to her husband, so long as he liveth *Rom. 2.2.*

Aged women should behave as becometh holi-
ness &c that they may teach the young women,
to be sober, to love their husbands, to love their
children, to be discreet keepers at home, good,
obedient to their own husbands. *Tit. 2. 3. 5.*

A promise of "I do"s
A flourish of wedding marches

A bond of weddings
A band of wedding rings
A thrill of brides
A thrall of bridegrooms
A standby of best men
A hover of maids-of-honor
A flutter of bridesmaids
A billow of bridal gowns
A shimmer of veils
A twitter of ring bearers
A shush of ushers

31

A "Smile!" of wedding pictures
A wave of wedding videos

A hint of bridal registries
A booty of wedding gifts
   But in certain circumstances:
A wedding gift of booties

An Everest of wedding cakes
A pop of flashbulbs
A rain of rice
A din of tin cans

A pomp of bridal suites
A romp of wedding nights

A June of honeymoons
A moon of nights
A spoon of days
A tune of love songs

A remembrance of anniversaries *(by women)*
An oversight of anniversaries *(by men)*
A sparkle of silver anniversaries
A glitter of golden anniversaries

A euphemism of significant others
A deconstruction of postmodern relationships

A pride of gay lovers

A trump of prenuptial agreements
  to guard against:
A no-trump of alimonies
  or
A slam of palimony suits

A skirmish of separations
A battle of divorces
A charge of divorce lawyers

A gambol of second marriages
A gamble of third marriages

A glimpse of décolletages
A convenience (*sometimes* inconvenience) of mistresses

A twist of trysts
A hothouse of love nests

A rage of maidens   An incredulity of cuckolds

These authentic terms of venery for maidens and cuckolds date from the list in The Book of St. Albans, rage in this case implying wantonness, and incredulity informing us that cuckolds haven't changed much in five hundred years.

A slouch of models

A score of bachelors

A freeze (*archaic:* frieze) of virgins

A parade of beauty queens

A wannabe of MAW's *(Model/Actress/Whatever)*

A dish of honeys
A cup of bosoms
A dash of pursuits
A pinch of posteriors
A pat of thighs
A drop of undies

A lump of sugar daddies
A dollop of dolls

A masquerade of personal ads
A chimera of Mister Rights
A mirage of Ms. Rights
A nudge of dating services
A push of matchmakers
A RAM of computerized dating services

A wander of husbands
A wonder of wives
A web of affairs

Formerly: A mews of cathouses
In the safe-sex era:
A condominium of massage parlors

MADAME 'IRMA'

An accommodation of escort services

An overflow of johns

A hangout of nudists

A spread of centerfolds

A grind of porn films

A groan of porn stars

A badinage of phone-sex numbers

An offal of obscene phone calls

A hang-up of heavy breathers

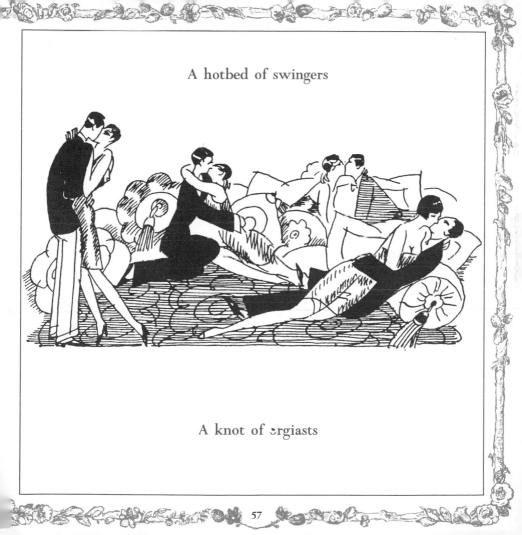

A hotbed of swingers

A knot of orgiasts

A layout of nymphomaniacs
A stand of studs
A dream of aphrodisiacs

A keyhole of voyeurs

A rack of sadomasochists
A smack of dominatrices

A nibble of foot fetishists

A crotchet of dirty old men
A phalanx of flashers

A vogue of cross-dressers
A trip of transsexuals
An ambivalence of bisexuals

The oldest profession provides us (appropriately) with one of the oldest terms of venery, a herd of harlots, which is the seventh term in the great St. Albans list, appearing two positions ahead of a bevy of ladies—and 125 positions ahead of a school of fish! Equally appropriate is the classic philological joke about the Oxford dons whose path is crossed by several prostitutes. "A jam of tarts," mutters the first don. Then, in succession, each of the dons makes a now-famous contribution to the game of venery:

A flourish of strumpets
An essay of Trollope's
An anthology of pros

A pride of loins
A peal of Jezebels
A smelting of ores

The game of venery lives. Play on!